Have You Ever Seen An Alaska Ermine?

Have You Ever Seen An Alaska Ermine?

BOB BENDA

ISBN-13: 9781519150172
ISBN-10: 1519150172

Have You Ever Seen An Alaska Ermine?

I live in Valdez, Alaska. I was at my property outside of town and heard what I thought was a bird calling. Suddenly an ermine appeared running around the tarp covered piles of lumber I store on the property. I had seen ermines in the winter with white fur, but I had never seen one with brown summer fur. I looked up information on ermines and found they are also called a stoat or a short-tailed weasel. The name ermine is often, but not always, used for the animal in its pure white winter coat. Most people would be lucky to see an ermine. They are swift, silent creatures and are mostly nocturnal (which means they spend most of their time moving and hunting at night). I was fortunate to be able to photograph ermines several times during the summer and fall. They move very fast and are difficult to photograph. Fortunately for me they are also curious and stopped many times to look at me. This photo is of the ermine I saw looking out at me from behind a black tarp.

It walked out from behind the black tarp and stood up on its hind legs. Ermine stand up so they can see more. This one was looking at me with my camera and large lens.

It dropped back down to look around. It stared at me and then moved to my left.

It ran to another pile of wood and turned around. It seemed to be trying to decide where to go next. I couldn't tell if this ermine was a male or female so I'll refer to the ermine as it.

It must have decided to run back to the other wood pile.

It stopped in the grass and looked at me again. I wasn't sure where it would go next.

It must have decided to run back to the other wood pile.

It stopped in the grass and looked at me again.
I wasn't sure where it would go next.

This is not a good photo, but is shows the ermine running away from me. It ran into nearby brush and disappeared.

I decided to go back the next day and see if the ermine might still be by the wood piles. Instead of one ermine I saw four of them running around the woodpiles. I assumed it was a mother and three young ones. The mother was probably the ermine I saw yesterday. The mother ermine rears the young with no help from the father. This photo shows two of the smaller ones inside a wooden pallet. One is looking out and you can just see the top of the other ermine's head and ear.

Now each ermine has a slot in the pallet. They are both looking out at me.

One of the young ermines left the pallet. An ermine's slender body allows it to move swiftly in underground burrows or in this instance through piles of wood. These photos were taken in early July. The female ermine gives birth sometime in April or May so these young ermine were between 8 to 12 weeks old.

It continued walking away from the pallet. The ermine's summer coat color is brown with white underbelly fur. The tip of the tail is black. The ermine's winter coat color is white, but the tip of the tail remains black.

It stopped and turned to look at me.

It started walking towards me. It looked directly at me as it was walking.

It stopped walking towards me and decided to look under a rock.

It looked over the rock at something. It might have been one of the other ermines. They were running all over the wood piles.

Another ermine went into the pallet. This ermine looked larger than the ermine in the pallet. Comparing its size with the smaller ermine I assumed it was the mother.

My assumption seemed to be correct. The mother ermine is rubbing noses with the smaller ermine.

While the mother ermine was in the pallet another smaller ermine emerged from under the black tarp. I don't know if this is one of the smaller ermines from the pallet or the other smaller one.

Mom came out from behind the pallet. She and the three young ermines left the woodpiles and ran off into the nearby brush. I went back several days hoping to see them again, but they were gone.

A few weeks later my wife told me she thought she saw a squirrel on our front porch. I looked at it and saw it was an ermine. I got my camera and hoped I would be able to take a few pictures of it. This photo shows it on our front porch.

This ermine was alone. After looking at me from the porch it ran on the driveway under the carport. Here it is standing next to my covered motorcycle.

It ran under the motorcycle cover and came out again.

It ran from the motorcycle cover and went under our Mitsubishi Montero Sport SUV. It stopped to look at me through the spokes of the tire rim.

The ermine ran up two flights of stairs to our carport deck. It stood up and looked around. In the woodlands, shrubs, fencerows, and open areas where they usually live ermine investigate every hole and crevice looking for something to eat. They often stop to survey their surroundings by standing upright on their hind legs.

It ran over to look under the flower barrel. Its image is reflected in the water on the deck.

It ran from the flower barrel across the carport deck carpets. You can see how it stretches out its body when it runs.

It ran down to a deck attached to the carport. It looked like it might be deciding to climb up the step.

It looked up at me from the top stair from the lower deck. Notice the pinkish nose on this ermine. The young ermines earlier in the book had brownish noses.

It jumped back on the carport deck. It stopped and started scratching itself.

The ermine ran from the carport deck to the driveway. It stopped under a bush at the end of the carport. It looked around before it ran off into the trees.

A few months later I was building a storage building at our son's house. I looked down from the ladder and saw an ermine in its white winter coat. I climbed down from the ladder, got my camera and I was able to take a few pictures. This photo shows it running. When ermines run they run in a series of leaps. Its flexible spine allows it to do the "marten run" in which the hind feet are tucked in by the front feet, causing the back to arch and then extend.

It stopped to look where it wanted to go next.

It ran into the grass and headed in the direction of the house.

The ermine stopped by the stairway and looked at me. It's standing by two old saws. It watched me for a little while then ran off into the brush behind the house.

Later this fall I was able to photograph another ermine at our house. It had acquired its white winter fur with the black tail tip. I don't know if this was the same ermine I took pictures of at our house this summer. This photo shows it by firewood stacked up under the carport.

It moved off the firewood and jumped down to the driveway. Its black tipped tail shows up well in this photo.

It ran under our Mitsubishi Montero Sport SUV parked under the carport. It has some pink on its nose so it might be the same ermine from this summer.

It ran down the driveway to the base of one of our Sitka Spruce trees.

The ermine started to run back towards our driveway. I thought it might run down the drive-way into the cul-de-sac or across the driveway into the other spruce trees.

It decided not to cross the driveway. It ran into the bushes near the spruce tree. That was the last time I saw the ermine by our house. I felt fortunate to have been able to photograph these ermine this year.

ALASKAN ERMINE FACT SHEET

1. Full adult size total body length is 170mm(6.8 inches) to 330mm(13.2 inches)
2. The tail length is about 35% of the total body length, ranging from 42 mm (1.7 inches) to 120 mm (4.8 inches).
3. Males are generally twice as large as females. Males weigh from 67g (2.3 ounces) to 116g (4.1 ounces). Females weigh from 25g (0.88 ounces) to 80g (2.8 ounces)
4. Ermines are found all over Canada, the northern USA, and Eurasia. They are not considered threatened or endangered.
5. Ermines have a white winter coat color and a brown and white summer color. The tip of their tail is always black.
6. Ermine prefer living in woodlands near rivers, marshes, shrubby fencerows and open areas next to forests or shrub borders.
7. Both male and female ermine have many different mates. Female produce only one litter per year. Litter size ranges from 3 to 18 young. The young can hunt with their mother by the eighth week. Female young can mate when they are 60 to 70 days old. Male young do not mate until their second summer.
8. Only females care for the young.
9. The average life span of ermines is 1 to 2 years in the wild. They can live to 7 years in captivity. Ermines are related to ferrets and other weasels.
10. Ermines are carnivores and hunt mostly at night. Their slender bodies allow them to search for prey in tunnels and burrows. They have 34 sharp teeth and kill their prey by biting the prey on the neck. They feed mostly on small mammals (mice, voles, lemmings, and rabbits), but will feed on birds, eggs, frogs, fish and insects if mammalian prey is scarce. Ermines have high energy demands and must eat daily. They do not hibernate and must feed year- round.

11. Ermines are preyed upon by foxes, American martens, fishers, American badgers, raptors (hawks, falcons, and owls), and domestic cats.
12. Ermine will prey on domestic fowl and chicken farmers do not like them.
13. The winter white colored fur was prized by religious leaders and British Royalty. They are still trapped today, but the demand for their pelts is on the decline in today's fashion market.
14. Ermines are very efficient small mammal predators (especially mice) which makes them valuable to humans.
15. You can find more information about ermines at http://www.biokids.umich.edu/critters/Mustela_erminea/